STUDY GUIDE
FOR
IT IS ALWAYS NOW!

MARDI LONG

Copyright © 2022 Mardi Long.

All rights reserved. No part of this book may be reproduced, stored, or transmitted by any means—whether auditory, graphic, mechanical, or electronic—without written permission of both publisher and author, except in the case of brief excerpts used in critical articles and reviews. Unauthorized reproduction of any part of this work is illegal and is punishable by law.

ISBN: 979-8-88640-073-1 (sc)
ISBN: 979-8-88640-074-8 (hc)
ISBN: 979-8-88640-075-5 (e)

Because of the dynamic nature of the Internet, any web addresses or links contained in this book may have changed since publication and may no longer be valid. The views expressed in this work are solely those of the author and do not necessarily reflect the views of the publisher, and the publisher hereby disclaims any responsibility for them.

One Galleria Blvd., Suite 1900, Metairie, LA 70001
1-888-421-2397

CONTENTS

Week One – Setting the Stage
Introduction 2
Free Will 6
The Kingdom Of God 10
The Path to Discovery 14

Week Two – Opening the Door
1. Open the Door 21
2. Seek and Focus 26

Week Three – Digging Deeper
3. Find and Grow 32
4. New Pathways 37

Week Four – The Rubber Hits the Road
5. Love! Judge Not 47
6. Transcend! 56

Week Five – The Road Beyond
Assured of Salvation? 61
Keep it Simple! 65
When in Doubt, Pray 69

APPENDIX

Appendix 1 For: Free Will 75
Appendix 2 For: The Kingdom of God 77
Appendix 3 For: The Path to Discovery 80
Appendix 4 For: 3. Find and Grow 84
Appendix 5 For: 5. Love – Judge Not! 86
Appendix 6 For: Keep It Simple 90
Appendix 7: Notes to the Discussion Leader(s) 92

SOURCES

BibleGateway.com: The Bible versions used [**KJV** and **NIV**].

Holy Bible, New International Version®, NIV® Copyright ©1973, 1978, 1984, 2011 by Biblica, Inc.® Used by permission in [**BibleGateway**.] All rights reserved worldwide.

NOTE: The King James Version of the Bible is largely considered to be public domain.

C. S. Lewis., *Mere Christianity* (Lewis Signature Classics) [**Lewis**]. UNKNOWN. Kindle Edition. [Pages are provided with each quote.] **NOTE**: All bolding, italicizing, and underlining of Lewis' works are my own.

Jamison, Fausset, Brown's Commentary on the Whole Bible [**Jamison**], 2971, Zondervan, New Addition (February 1, 1999)

Frederic and Mary Ann Brussat, *100 Ways to Keep Your Soul Alive* [**100 Ways**], Harper One, 1994

Mardi Long, *It Is Always Now* [**IIAN**], Published though the Amazon Kindle Self Publishing app. 2020

Plus my additional **OBSERVATIONS** not in IIAN

PREFACE

Why am I writing this book? Because there is so much more behind *It Is Always NOW*.

Why write it in this manner – using references to these other works?

Because *It Is Always NOW* is all I have got. I simply do not know how to expand on it. It is what is in my heart. I can't seem to find the words to explain it more fully.

Note that this is **not** intended to be a theological work. It is meant to open discussion. You don't agree with some of my references? Great – talk about them. Why do you not agree? That is a good thing.

This is an effort to "fill in the blanks" or to "tell the rest of the story." I am pulling these determinations of others together. The ones that have helped to solidify and strengthen for me what is in my heart.

Words **are** important. Not in and of themselves. But because they do, over time, shape who you are. Because they trigger new insights and understandings. Think about it. One little word, used in the right way, at the right time and the right place, can cause an explosion of thought and understanding.

So read this for what it is worth. But never, ever just take someone else's word for it. Study for yourself. Seek that balance between heart and mind and soul. These things together become the very essence of who you are.

NEVER stop opening your heart to the Joy!

NEVER stop seeking – always with an open mind!

If you just do those two things you **will** find something that is more precious than gold.

NOTE TO PARTICIPANTS

Thank you for coming on this journey. You will benefit most if you read the materials, keep a journal, participate in the discussions, and pray.

It is my prayer that you will find some insights and encouragement. Keep an open heart and follow where the journey leads you. This is a journey that must keep evolving throughout your lifetime. And no two journeys are the same. It is not always easy to be sure. But I believe you will find it is well worth the effort.

So here we go. No pressure….. One step at a time……

WEEK ONE

SETTING THE STAGE

INTRODUCTION

Personal Discovery

IIAN: Everyone must realize their own journey. [Introduction]

Dear Fellow Traveler,

Is it just me, or is our digital world the very epitome of information overload? How do we sort through the constant and often conflicting information that rushes at us every day? I have found it to be so much easier with a solid, personal belief system in place.

If you have read *It Is Always NOW*, you already know the general direction I am heading. But many have asked for a little more. And that is what *The Study Guide* attempts to provide. I have written this because I understand the desire for more substance. But, please! You must always remember that this is *your* journey. No one has all of the answers. Some things can never be fully understood in this life. With the Joy and Sunshine in your heart and mind, always evaluate for yourself. And never, ever lose that spark of curiosity!

Mardi

TALKING POINTS:

- Digital world – information overload

- Personal belief system - balance

- Personal journey – what's curiosity got to do with it?

100 Ways – p. 2 - *Introduction*

- Keeping your soul alive is an adventure, a delightful challenge, a rousing responsibility, and an essential spiritual practice.

- The phrase first leaped out at us from the pages of a 1990 novel, J. M. Coetzee's *Age of Iron*. The Protagonist, a retired classics professor in South Africa, writes to his daughter: "I am trying to keep my soul alive in times not hospitable to soul."

100 Ways – #98 – *Groom Your Curiosity*

- It began as a mystery, and it will end in mystery, but what a savage and beautiful country lies in between. *Diane Ackerman in A Natural History of the Senses*

FREE WILL

Foundation of the Universe

IIAN: …"free will" is the foundation of God's universe.

LEWIS: The Shocking Alternative

"God created things which had free will. That means creatures which can go either wrong or right. Some people think they can imagine a creature which was free but had no possibility of going wrong; I cannot. If a thing is free to be good it is also free to be bad. And free will is what has made evil possible. Why, then, did God give them free will? Because free will, though it makes evil possible, is also the only thing that makes possible any love or goodness or joy worth having. A world of automata—of creatures that worked like machines—would hardly be worth creating. The happiness which God designs for His higher creatures is the happiness of being freely, voluntarily united to Him and to each other in an ecstasy of love and delight compared with which the most rapturous love between a man and a woman on this earth is mere milk and water. And for that they must be free." [Location 600, page 42]

TALKING POINTS

- Only you can let God in.

- What can happen when you let Him in?

- Why we so often go "wrong" – lose our focus?

SEE APPENDIX 1: PAGE 75

100 Ways - # 52 – *Just Do It*

- A young salesman approached the farmer and began talking excitedly about the book he was carrying. "This book will tell you everything you need to know about farming"…

- "Young man," the farmer said, "that's not the problem. I know everything in that book. My problem is doing it." Joseph Gosse in *Spiritual Life* magazine

OBSERVATION: Only we can "make" ourselves do something. That is free will. Knowledge alone does not save us from ourselves. We need strength from beyond ourselves to do the things that really count.

Mark 9:24
24Immediately the boy's father exclaimed, "I do believe; help me overcome my unbelief!" [NIV]

John 10:10
10The thief comes only to steal and kill and destroy; I have come that they may have life, and have it to the full. [NIV]

THE KINGDOM OF GOD

Here and Now

IIAN: The Kingdom of God is here and now – as much as is humanly possible in this life.

LEWIS:

"If you want to get warm you must stand near a fire…. If you want joy, power, peace, eternal life, you must get close to, or even into, the thing that has them…. There are a great fountain of energy and beauty spurting up that the very centre of reality… Once a man is united to God, how could he not live forever?"
[Page 133, Location 1962]

OBSERVATIONS:

- Why do I bring these things up at the beginning of the book? Because I find that unless you really understand the goal or map, you will never quite understand why the steps are necessary. If you are reading this book, you are seeking a deeper experience. Yes?

- When Jesus says "the kingdom is at hand" I believe He was referring to the fact that once He completed his mission, rose from the dead, and returned to His Father, everything would be (and has ever since been) done to reclaim this world. After that, "the kingdom" would be available to us – as it is here and now – for the taking. God's Kingdom is ALWAYS available to us for the taking.

- Of course, our final destination and our final rebirth is yet to come….

TALKING POINTS:

- Read IIAN page 2
- Read I John 3:1,2
- The goal
- What does "Kingdom at hand" mean?
- What has PRAISE got to do with it?
- Read IIAN p. 2

CHALLENGE: How many words can you think of that are related to PRAISE?

CHALLENGE: This coming week, see how many references you can find to "The Kingdom" in the Gospels.

SEE APPENDIX 2: PAGE 77

THE PATH TO DISCOVERY

Always a Work In-Progress

IIAN: Each step builds on the one before. [Page 3]

LEWIS:

"…a Christian can lose the Christ-life which has been put into him, and he has to make efforts to keep it." [Page 53, Location 770]

"But the Christian thinks any good he does comes from the Christ-life inside him. He does not think God will love us because we are good, but that God will make us good because He loves us; just as the roof of a greenhouse does not attract the sun because it is bright, but becomes bright because the sun shines on it." [Page 54, Location 778]

"Neither this belief nor any other will automatically remain alive in the mind. It must be fed. And as a matter of fact, if you examined a hundred people who had lost their faith in Christianity, I wonder how many of them would turn out to have been reasoned out of it by honest argument? Do not most people simply drift away?" [Page 109, Location 1604]

HOW IT WORKS

1. First you must open the door of your heart and claim the **JOY** of the Lord. This is what inspires you and drives you forward. Repeat every day!

2. As you seek and focus on The Word and truths that the Joy guides you to, God will fill you with enduring **LOVE** [in] that can only come from Him.

3. Persevere calmly and with constant prayer to find abiding **PEACE** and grow in the deeper truths that are there for the asking and taking.

4. As you allow the Joy to work within you, you will find truths – together with abundant **HOPE** - that can only come from a daily walk with our Lord. This will allow the Joy to reinvent new pathways [in your mind, heart, and soul] on your daily journey to the ultimate Kingdom of God.

5. You must constantly struggle to develop (and hold onto) that abiding **FAITH** so you will be able to accept that God alone is the judge and that your job as a Christian is to just **LOVE** [out] others.

6. You must set no limit to what you believe our Lord can do for you and in you. Even in this life you can **TRANSCEND** and experience rapture in the presence of the Joy. If only for brief moments in time.

SETTING A COURSE FOR THE JOURNEY

- Think of a 1000 piece puzzle. The box provides a picture of the finished product. But it takes a long time to find and place each of the tiny pieces. Sometimes you want to walk away and forget it. But the potential of the feeling of the satisfaction of getting to the end drives you on.

- Now think of a 1000 piece puzzle that comes with no picture. That is how life feels sometimes. But the God who created us has provided a picture. His life on earth together with our own experiences and input from so many other sources. The little tiny pieces, experiences, events of our existence often seem overwhelming. Just remember:

- Romans 8:28: **28**And we know that in all things God works for the good of those who love him, who[a] have been called according to his purpose. [NIV]

TALKING POINTS

- Work-in-progress…

- The process never ends.

- We do not walk alone.

HINT: Getting these steps in the right order will make your journey much easier.

CHALLENGE: Pick one of the key words for PRAISE [Page 16] and look up some of the verses in the Bible that use those words.

SEE APPENDIX 3: PAGE 80

100 Ways - *# 17 – Be Open to Epiphanies*

- An epiphany is a sudden realization of a significant truth, usually arising out of a commonplace event. At that special moment, a life meaning becomes clear to you – an insight into your personality, a discovery of something you value or believe in, and an acute sense of where you are in life…. Such moments can determine the course for your life as much as your response to a crisis. Robert U. Akeret with Daniel Klein in *Family Tales, Family Wisdom*

WEEK TWO

OPENING THE DOOR

Psalm 89:15
Blessed are those who have learned to acclaim you, who walk in the light of your presence, Lord. [NIV]

Philippians 4:6
⁶Do not be anxious about anything, but in every situation, by prayer and petition, with thanksgiving, present your requests to God. ⁷And the peace of God, which transcends all understanding, will guard your hearts and your minds in Christ Jesus. [NIV]

1. OPEN THE DOOR

Relax, Grow & Glow

IIAN: It all has to start with Joy! [Page 5]

LEWIS:

"What the scientists believe is a mathematical formula. The pictures are there only to help you to understand the formula. They are not really true in the way the formula is; they do not give you the real thing but only something more or less like it. They are meant to help. And if they do not help you we do not understand it."

"<u>A man can eat his dinner without understanding exactly how food nourishes him.</u> A man can accept what Christ has done without knowing how it works: indeed, he certainly would not know how it works until he has accepted it." [Page 28, Location 690]

TALKING POINTS:

- What is the Joy and Sunshine as I used it in IIAN?

- Why use symbolism?

- You might say, "But I don't understand it all..." and that is OK ☺.

- [Grains of sand]

CHALLENGE: What words would you use to describe the Joy?

100 Ways – # 15 – *Be Spiritually Inebriated*

- Spiritual inebriation is this: that a man receives more sensible joy and sweetness than his heart can either contain or desire. Spiritual inebriation brings forth many strange gestures in men. It makes them sing and praise God because of their fulness of joy, and some weep with great tears because of the sweetness of heart. It makes one restless in all his limbs, so that he must run and jump and dance; and so excites another that he must gesticulate and clap his hands. John of Ruysbroeck quoted in *The Common Experience*

100 Ways - # 85 – *Moments of Happiness*

- I've been thinking about happiness – how wrong it is ever to expect it to last or there to be a time of happiness. It's not that, it's a moment of happiness. Almost every day containing at least one moment of happiness. May Sarton in *Endgame*

NOTES:

Matthew 6:6

⁶But when you pray, go into your room, close the door and pray to your Father, who is unseen. Then your Father, who sees what is done in secret, will reward you. [NIV]

Matthew 7:7
Ask, Seek, Knock
⁷"Ask and it will be given to you; seek and you will find; knock and the door will be opened to you. [NIV]

2. SEEK AND FOCUS

Your Secret Garden

IIAN: Having a set time and place to study will increase your chance of success.

LEWIS:

"Besides being complicated, reality, in my experience is usually odd. It is not neat, not obvious, not what you expect." [Page 37, Location 534]

IIAN: "Very little in life is black and white. That is why we must constantly keep our hearts and minds open." [Page 7]

1 Corinthians 13:12
For **now we see through** a glass, darkly; but then face to face: **now** I know in part; but then shall I know even as also I am known. [NIV]

TALKING POINTS:

- Why study and pray every day?

- Why read the Bible?

- What about other books/sources?

- Do you have a favorite song that you might share with us?

CHALLENGE: Find a new verse each week. Write it in your notebook. Read it every day. Just one or two verses.

100 Ways - # 16 – *Have a Beginner's Mind*

- If your mind is empty, it is always ready for anything; it is open to everything. In the beginner's mind there are **many possibilities**, in the expert's mind there are few. Shunryu Suzuki-Roshi in *Zen Mind, Beginner's Mind*

OBSERVATION: Of course, we do not want or need to disregard what we already know. But we must ever remember that even when it comes to the "basics," there is always more to learn at that level as well. Even if we consider ourselves to be a Biblical "expert," we must remember that we can never know "everything" about anything. And for "the record" – I am **not** a Biblical "expert!"

NOTES:

WEEK THREE

DIGGING DEEPER

Romans 11:33

Doxology

[33]Oh, the depth of the riches of the wisdom and[a] knowledge of God! How unsearchable his judgments, and his paths beyond tracing out! [NIV]

3. FIND AND GROW

Wonder Wisely

Psalm 10:1-6 [NIV]

Psalm 10

[1]Why, Lord, do you stand far off?
    Why do you hide yourself in times of trouble?
[2]In his arrogance the wicked man hunts down
    the weak, who are caught in the schemes
    he devises.
[3]He boasts about the cravings of his heart;
    he blesses the greedy and reviles the LORD.
[4]In his pride the wicked man does not seek him;
    in all his thoughts there is no room for God.
[5]His ways are always prosperous;
    your laws are rejected by[b] him;
    he sneers at all his enemies.
[6]He says to himself, "Nothing will ever shake me."
    He swears, "No one will ever do me harm."

IIAN: Do not rush it – let it happen one step at a time. [Page 9]

LEWIS:

"Now what was the sort of "hole" man had got himself into? He had tried to set up on his own, to behave as if he belonged to himself. In other words, <u>fallen man</u> is not simply an imperfect creature who needs improvement: he <u>is a rebel who must lay down his arms.</u> Laying down your arms, surrendering, saying you are sorry, realizing that you have been on the wrong track and getting ready to start life over again from the ground floor – that is the only way out of our "hole." This process of surrender – this movement full speed astern – is what Christians call repentance. It is something much harder than merely eating humble pie. It means <u>unlearning all the self-conceit and self-will</u> that we have been training ourselves into for thousands of years." [Page 49, Location 703]

TALKING POINTS:

- What does "milk and meat" say to you?

- How much "meat" is required for our salvation?

CHALLENGE: Think of one example of "milk" and one example of "meat."

SEE APPENDIX 4: PAGE 84

100 Ways - # 50 – *Live in Awe*

- Awe enables us to perceive in the world intimations of the divine, to sense in small things the beginning of infinite significance, to sense the ultimate in the common and the simple; to feel in the rush of the passing the stillness of the eternal. Abraham Joshua Heschel in *The Wisdom of Heschel*

100 Ways - # 64 – *Recognize Magic*

- Magic is a sudden opening of mind to the wonder of existence. It is a sense that there is much more to life than we usually recognize; that we do not have to be confined by the limited views of our family, our society, or our own habitual thoughts impose on us; that life contains many dimensions, depths, textures, and meaning extending far beyond our familiar beliefs and concepts. John Welwood in *Ordinary Magic*

NOTES:

Isaiah 42:16

16I will lead the blind by ways they have not known,
    along unfamiliar paths I will guide them;
I will turn the darkness into light before them
    and make the rough places smooth.
These are the things I will do;
    I will not forsake them. [NIV]

4. NEW PATHWAYS

Be Not Afraid

Colossians 1:13

13For he has rescued us from the dominion of darkness and brought us into the kingdom of the Son he loves. [NIV]

Romans 12:2

2Do not conform to the pattern of this world, but be transformed by the renewing of your mind. Then you will be able to test and approve what God's will is—his good, pleasing and perfect will. [NIV]

IIAN: Yes, **REINVENT** *a new us!* (p. 11)

LEWIS:
ON "THE THREE PERSONAL GOD"

"What I mean is this. An ordinary simple Christian kneels down to say his prayers. He is trying to get into touch with God.

But if he is a Christian he knows that what is prompting him to pray is also God: God, so to speak, inside him.

But he also knows that all the real knowledge of God comes through Christ, the Man who was God – that Christ [through the Joy we allow in] is standing beside him, helping him to pray, praying for him.

You see what is happening. God [God the Father] is the thing to which he is praying – the goal he is trying to reach.

God is also the thing inside him [the Joy] which is pushing him on – the motivating power.

God is also the road or bridge [Jesus Christ] along which he is being pushed to that goal."

KVE

Colossians 1:13

Who hath delivered us from the power of darkness, and hath **translated** us into the kingdom of his dear Son:

Hebrews 11:5

By faith Enoch was **translated** that he should not see death; and was not found, because God had **translated** him: for before his translation he had this testimony, that he pleased God.

NIV

Romans 12:2

Do not conform to the pattern of this world, but be **transformed** by the renewing of your mind. Then you will be able to test and approve what God's will is—his good, pleasing and perfect will.

2 Corinthians 3:18

And we all, who with unveiled faces contemplate the Lord's glory, are being **transformed** into his image with ever-increasing glory, which comes from the Lord, who is the Spirit.

ABOUT YOUR "GLASS"

- When you feel those destructive **old pathways** (feelings and emotions) bubbling up and taking over

STOP!   REFOCUS!

- Take a deep breath. Let the Joy in and seek and claim the calm feelings and emotions – **the new pathways** - that the Lord is slowly building in you.

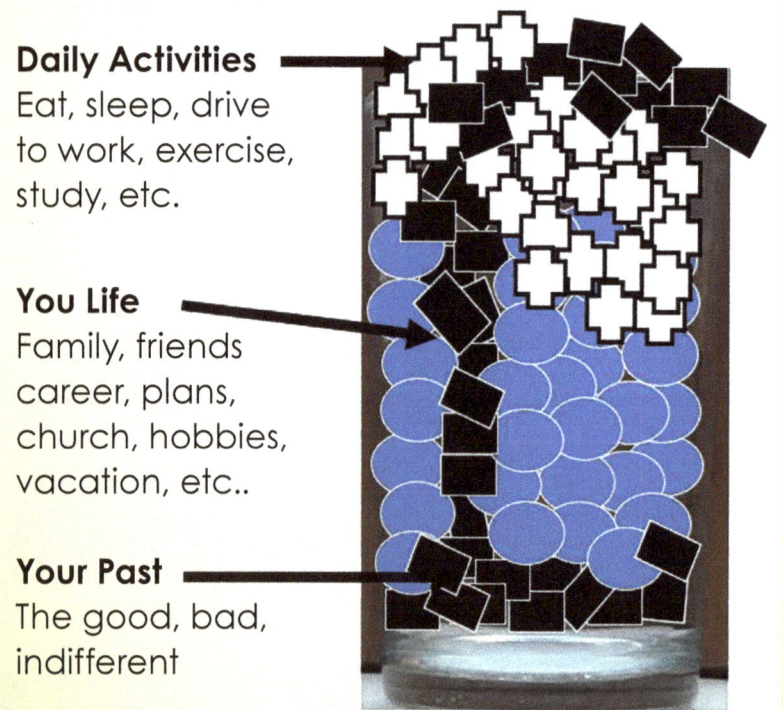

Daily Activities
Eat, sleep, drive to work, exercise, study, etc.

You Life
Family, friends career, plans, church, hobbies, vacation, etc..

Your Past
The good, bad, indifferent

> What your glass looks like when your past is not in perspective and things in your current life are out of control.
>
> You lose control. You do not have the capacity to deal with daily activities. This leads to misplaced anger like road rage, for example.

What your glass looks like when your past is in perspective and things in your current life are going along quite smoothly.

REMEMBER: No one's glass is **ever** entirely perfect in this life! But the closer our connection to the Joy – the closer we get to a stable presence of heart and mind.

100 Ways - #25 – Don't Make Comparisons

Everybody is unique. Compare not yourself with Anybody else lest you spoil God's curriculum.
Baal Shem Tov

SELF DISCIPLINE

- Think athletes, serious students, body builders, dieters, and on and on….

- They do not go to the gym once or twice and then sit on the sofa all day or lose weight and then stop thinking about what they eat.

- So why are we so surprised that a walk with The Lord – which is far more important – also requires constant/consistent self discipline??

- This needs to be more important to us than our daily shower.

TALKING POINTS:

- Habits

- Never give up!

- Remember Moses.

OBSERVATION: Our bad habits create static that prevents us from being able to feel and respond to the Joy. We the Joy, the Sunshine.

CHALLENGE: Think of one habit you know you need to change. Write it on a single page in your notebook. Do not show it to anyone. Pray about it this week.

100 Ways - # 29 – *Exercise Your Imagination*

- Imagination has the creative task of making symbols, joining things together in such a way that they throw new light on each other and on everything around them. The imagination is a discovering faculty, a faculty for seeing relationships, for seeing meanings that are special and even quite new. Thomas Merton in *Contemplation in a World of Action*

100 Ways - # 39 – *Don't Try to See Through the Distances*

- Keep walking, though there's no place to get to. Don't try to see through the distances. That's not for human beings. Move within, but don't move the way fear makes you move. Rumi in *Unseen Rain, Quatrains of Rumi*

NOTES:

WEEK FOUR

THE RUBBER HITS THE ROAD

Romans 13:8
Love Fulfills the Law
⁸Let no debt remain outstanding, except the point weighed six hundred shekels.[a] His shield continuing debt to love one another, for bearer went ahead of him. [NIV]

1 Samuel 17:7
⁷His spear shaft was like a weaver's rod, and its iron
whoever loves others has fulfilled the law. [NIV]

Luke 6:37
Judging Others
³⁷Do not judge, and you will not be judged. Do not condemn, and you will not be condemned. Forgive, and you will be forgiven. [NIV]

5. LOVE! JUDGE NOT

Phone a Friend!

IIAN: Have Faith – God is the judge. (p. 13)

LEWIS: ON LOVE:

- **"Do not waste time bothering whether you "love" your neighbour; act as if you did.** As soon as we do this we find one of the great secrets. When you are behaving as if you loved someone, you will presently come to love him. If you injure someone you dislike, you will find yourself disliking him more. If you do him a good turn, you will find yourself disliking him less.

- There is, indeed, one exception. If you do him a good turn, not to please God and obey the low of charity (aka love), but to show him what a fine forgiving chap you are, and to put him in your debt, and then sit down to wait for his "gratitude," you will probably be disappointed...."
[Page 101 Location 1495 and 14497]

OBSERVATION: And I might add.....Miss the whole point and make it rather impossible to be right with God.

LEWIS: ON FORGIVENESS

"<u>Everyone says forgiveness is a lovely idea, until they have something to forgive, as we did during the war...</u>

[You ask] 'I wonder how you would feel about forgiving the Gestapo if you were a Pole or a Jew?'

"'Forgive us our sins as we forgive those that sin against us.' There is no slightest suggestion that we are offered forgiveness on any other terms. It is made perfectly clear that if we do not forgive we shall not be forgiven. There are not two ways about it. What are we to do?..." [Page 89 Location 1318]

MY SUMMARY of what HE GOES ON TO SAY:

- **We must start with ourselves.** We loathe some of the things we have done. But we must still realize that God forgives us and we must love ourselves as the children of God that we are.

- **We can then also loathe the actions of others.** But realize that God does love them, too. He died for them, too. We can hope and pray that they may find forgiveness and find the love God offers to all.

WHAT JESUS SAID:

Luke 6:37

37Judge not, and ye shall not be judged: condemn not, and ye shall not be condemned: forgive, and ye shall be forgiven: [JKV]

WHAT FRANCIS OF ASSISI SAID:

Preach the gospel every day.
If necessary, use words.

2 Peter 3:9

The Lord is not slack concerning his promise, as some men count slackness; but is longsuffering to us-ward, not willing **that any should perish**, but **that** all **should** come to repentance. [KJV]

OBSERVATION: Could it be that we are ALL predestined to be saved?

Getting these steps in the right order will make your journey much easier.

OBSERVATION: Think about this. Can you truly forgive someone unless you love them? Can you truly love them unless you have the Joy of God's love in your heart?

OBSERVATIONS:

- Now do you see why I say that the order of the steps matters?

- Again, think of your relationship with other people. You have to "build" that relationship over time. You say things like, "I love you" or "You have no idea how much I value our relationship."

- Over time you become "soul mates" and learn what is really important to them. You learn about their past, their dreams, their deepest desires and thoughts. You are "committed" and you are "there" for each other.

- But no matter how "deep" the relationship becomes, you always need to remind them – and yourself – of how much you care. You always need to keep that early spark of amazement that you felt as your relationship began.

TALKING POINTS:

- Judging who?

- Judging what?

- The forgiveness factor

- Why is this step 5? Shouldn't it come sooner – maybe first?

CHALLENGE: On a single page in your notebook, write something down that you are struggling to forgive. Pray about it this next week.

SEE APPENDIX 5: PAGE 86

100 Ways - # 10 – **Distinguish the Dawn**

- An old rabbi once asked his pupils how they could tell when night had ended and the day had begun.

[The pupils came up with several ideas that the rabbi rejected.]

- "Then, what is it?" the pupils demanded.

- "It is when you can look on the face of any man or woman and see that it is your sister or brother. Because if you cannot see this, it is still night." Scott Russell Sanders in *Staying Put*

100 Ways - # 3 – *Be Kind*

- We cannot make the Kingdom of God happen, but we can put out leaves as it draws near. We can be kind to each other. We can drive back the darkness a little. We can make green places within ourselves and among ourselves where God can make his Kingdom happen.
  Frederik Buechner in *The Clown in he Belfry*

NOTES:

Psalm 39:3
³my heart grew hot within me. While I meditated, the fire burned; then I spoke with my tongue: [NIV]

Psalm 63:6
⁶On my bed I remember you;
I think of you through the watches of the night. [NIV]

6. TRANSCEND!

Set No Limits!

Matthew 17:1-7
The Transfiguration
¹⁷After six days Jesus took with him Peter, James and John the brother of James, and led them up a high mountain by themselves. ²There he was transfigured before them. His face shone like the sun, and his clothes became as white as the light. ³Just then there appeared before them Moses and Elijah, talking with Jesus.

⁴Peter said to Jesus, "Lord, it is good for us to be here. If you wish, I will put up three shelters—one for you, one for Moses and one for Elijah."

⁵While he was still speaking, a bright cloud covered them, and a voice from the cloud said, "This is my Son, whom I love; with him I am well pleased. Listen to him!"

⁶When the disciples heard this, they fell facedown to the ground, terrified. ⁷But Jesus came and touched them. "Get up," he said. "Don't be afraid." [NIV]

IIAN: Why are we so afraid of Meditation? (p. 15)

LEWIS: on "the presence of God"

"The real test of being in the presence of God is that you .. Forget about yourself altogether." [Page 97 Location 1428]

"…when the anesthetic fog which we call "nature" or "the real world" fades away and the Presence in which you have always stood becomes palpable, immediate, and unavoidable…." [Page 161 Location 2388 of 2391]

"Now, if you care to talk in these terms, the Christian view is precisely that the Next Step has already appeared. And it is really new. It is not a change from a brainy man to brainier men: it is a change that goes off in a totally different direction – <u>a change from being creatures of God to being sons of God</u>." [Page 163 Location 2416

TALKING POINTS:

- What have feelings got to do with it?

- Preconceived notions – not allowed….

CHALLENGE: Use BibleGateway to see how many references there are in the Bible to *meditation*.

NOTES:

WEEK FIVE

THE ROAD BEYOND

John 10:9
[9]I am the gate; whoever enters through me will be
saved.[a] They will come in and go out, and find pasture. [NIV]

Ephesians 1:5-6
[5]he[a] predestined us for adoption to sonship[b] through Jesus Christ, in accordance with his pleasure and will—[6]to the praise of his glorious grace, which he has freely given us in the One he loves. [NIV]

ASSURED OF SALVATION?

What the Bible Teaches

IIAN: The Shepherd is always there.... (p. 17)

LEWIS:

[Note: Lewis only uses the word "**salvation**" 3 times]

"The Bible really seems to clinch the matter when it puts the two things together [faith and works] into one amazing sentence."
[Page 114 Location 1689]

"The first half is, "Work out your own **salvation** with fear and trembling" – which looks as if everything depended on us and our good actions: but the second half goes on, 'For it is God who woketh in you" – which looks as if God did everything and we nothing.'"
[Page 114 Location 1690]

"Humanity is already "saved" in principle. We individuals have to appropriate [accept, internalize] that salvation. But the really tough work – the bit we could not have done for ourselves – has already been done for us."
[Page 136 Location 2015]

"A world of nice people, content in their own niceness, looking no further, turned away from God, would be just as desperately in need of **salvation** as a miserable world – and might be even more difficult to save."
[Page 160 Location 2378]

TALKING POINTS:

- Yes

- But….

- Stay connected

- Can you help someone that does not want your help – or thinks they do not need help?

CHALLENGE: Ask yourself, "Why is it so difficult to accept the gift, the salvation, that God so freely offers us?"

NOTES:

2 Samuel 23:4

⁴he is like the light of morning at sunrise
    on a cloudless morning,
like the brightness after rain
    that brings grass from the earth.' [NIV]

Luke 11:36

³⁶Therefore, if your whole body is full of light, and no part of it dark, it will be just as full of light as when a lamp shines its light on you." [NIV]

KEEP IT SIMPLE!

Plug into the Joy – New Each Morning

IIAN: Open the door! (p. 17)

LEWIS:

"In other words, fallen man is not simply an imperfect creature who needs improvement: he is a rebel who must lay down his arms. Laying down your arms, surrendering, saying you are sorry, realizing that you have been on the wrong track and getting ready to start life over again from the ground floor – that is the only way out of the "hole. This process of surrender – this movement full speed astern – is what Christians call repentance. Now **repentance is no fun at all**."
[Page 49 Location 107]

"Remember, this repentance, this willing submission to humiliation and a kind of death, is not something God demands of you before He will take you back and which He could let you off if He chose: it is simply a description of what going back to Him is like."
[Page 49 Location 710]

"God will love us because we are good, but that God will make us good because He loves us." [Page 54 Location 778]

OBSERVATION: It means accepting that you can do nothing on your own! It is never "your turn." You can never go on autopilot. You can never take complete control. As soon as you do – down you go!

TALKING POINTS:

- Focus on the basics.

- Keep your heart and mind open to new insights.

- It is Always NOW!

CHALLENGE: Think of something you do not want to let go of. Something you do not want to let God do for you. Write it down. Pray about it.

SEE APPENDIX 6: PAGE 90

NOTES:

Psalm 27:14 [NIV]
¹⁴Wait for the LORD;
be strong and take heart
and wait for the LORD.

Luke 244:38
He said to them, "Why are you troubled, and why do **doubt**s rise in your minds? [NIV]

WHEN IN DOUBT, PRAY

Then "...wait for the Lord" Psalm 27:14

IIAN: Just wait and follow...God will find you! (p. 19)

LEWIS:

"The only things we can keep are the things we freely give to God." [Page 158 Location 2346]

"The perfect surrender and humiliation were undergone by Christ: perfect because He was God, surrender and humiliation because He was man." [Page 51 Location 737]

"The more we get what we now call "ourselves" out of the way and let Him take us over, the more truly ourselves we become." [Page 167 Location 2477)

> "The more I resist Him and try to live on my own, the more I become dominated by my own heredity and upbringing and surroundings and natural desires. In fact what I so proudly call 'Myself.'" [Page 167 Location 2480]

TALKING POINTS:

- You will have doubts.

- These doubts can be stumbling blocks.

- OR

- A reminder that you need to….. "**Wait** for the Lord" - what does that mean? [Read page 19 in IIAN]

NEVER FORGET!

> "God does nothing prematurely, but, foreseeing the end from the beginning, waits till all is ripe for the execution of His purpose!"
> [Jamison]

Location 17849

Isaiah 12:2

Surely, it is God who saves me; I will trust in him and not be afraid.

For the Lord is my stronghold and my sure defense, and he will be my Savior.

[NIV]

APPENDIX

When I was a young child, I used to go to church with my grandmother. I had my paper I could draw and color on. But, I was listening. Even as an adult, I often recall the lessons I learned there. One lesson in particular has become a favorite go-to when I get too full of myself. And understand that much of my childhood was spent on the northern Oregon coast where we had miles of sandy beaches.

The pastor said something like this: "When you are on the beach think of the tiny grains of sand on that endless beach. Too many to count or begin to imagine. That is all the knowledge in God's universe. Now, scoop up a handful of dry sand and watch the grains trickle through your fingers. What you have left in the palm of your hand is all the knowledge that we humans have available to us in this lifetime."

APPENDIX 1 FOR: FREE WILL

SEE TALKING POINTS: PAGE 8

LEWIS: about the "DARK POWER?"

"How did the Dark Power go wrong? Here, no doubt, we ask a question to which human beings cannot give an answer with any certainty. A reasonable (and traditional) guess… can, however, be offered. The moment you have a self at all, there is a possibility of putting yourself first – wanting to be the center – wanting to be God, in fact. That was the sin of Satan: and that was the sin he taught the human race…. What Satan put into the heads of our remote ancestors was the idea that they could 'be like gods"…" [Page 46 Location 618]

NOTE: If you want to find out how Lewis sees the way Satan is constantly trying to pull us away from God, read his book *The Screwtape Letters*.

NOTE: If you believe that "Satan" is not an actual being, that is fine. But as an author, I feel it is appropriate to present different views. It is up to each individual to determine for themselves. The basic principles still apply.

APPENDIX 2 FOR:
THE KINGDOM OF GOD

SEE TALKING POINTS: PAGE 13

Matthew 3:2

And saying, Repent ye: for **the kingdom** of heaven is at hand. [KJV]

Matthew 5:3

Blessed are **the** poor in spirit: for **the**irs is **the kingdom** of heaven. [KJV]

Matthew 6:33

But seek ye first **the kingdom** of God, and his righteousness; and all **the**se things shall be added unto you. [KJV]

1 John 3:1-2

¹Behold, what manner of love the Father hath bestowed upon us, that we should be called the sons of God: therefore the world knoweth us not, because it knew him not. ² Beloved, now are we the sons of God, and it doth not yet appear what we shall be: but we know that, when he shall appear, we shall be like him; for we shall see him as he is. [KJV]

Synonyms for Praise

- Bless
- Carol/Hymn
- Celebrate
- Emblazon
- Exalt
- Extol
- Glorify
- Laud
- Magnify
- Resound

Words Related to PRAISE

- Adore
- Belaud
- Deify
- Worship
- Adulate
- Idolize
- Eulogize
- Acclaim
- Magnify
- Applaud

APPENDIX 3 FOR:
THE PATH TO DISCOVERY

SEE TALKING POINTS: PAGE 18

NIV

- **JOY – 242**

- LOVE [in] – 686

- PEACE – 249

- HOPE – 180

- FAITH – 458 – LOVE [out]

- TRANSCEND – 1 (0)

KJV

- **JOY – 187**

- LOVE [in] – 442

- CHARITY – 24

- PEACE – 420

- HOPE – 133

- FAITH – 336 – LOVE [out]

- TRANSCEND – 0

The End Game

The greatest ignominy (shame, disgrace) of the human condition is that we learn too little, too late - and we do so much damage while learning it….. The only antidote to this deplorable (unfortunate) state of affairs is to keep the THE JOY ever in our minds and hearts!!

Only God can right the wrongs already facilitated and guide in such in such a way as to avoid future ones.

OBSERVATIONS:

- This is really no different than a relationship with another person in your life – say a life partner or a longtime friend. If we do not constantly communicate and express our love and caring for them, the relationship will eventually weaken and even cease to exist. How often do people who get divorced say, "The marriage was over a long time ago."

- That is the basis of sayings like, "People who pray together, stay together." Or, "People who play together, stay together." Both concepts are important. If we really want a close relationship with a loved one, we must engage in every aspect of our lives.

- So we must take time each day to grow in our relationship with God.

APPENDIX 4 FOR:
3. FIND AND GROW

SEE TALKING POINTS: PAGE 34

PAUL'S PRAYER FOR THE EPHESIANS 3:14-21 [KJV]

May this be MY daily prayer!

[14] For this cause I bow my knees unto the Father of our Lord Jesus Christ,

[15] Of whom the whole family in heaven and earth is named,

[16] That he would grant you, according to the riches of his glory, to be strengthened with might by his Spirit in the inner man;

[17] That Christ may dwell in your hearts by faith; that ye, being rooted and grounded in love,

[18] May be able to comprehend with all saints what is the breadth, and length, and depth, and height;

[19] **And to know the love of Christ, which passeth knowledge, that ye might be filled with all the fulness of God.**

[20] Now unto him that is able to do exceeding abundantly above all that we ask or think, according to the power that worketh in us,

[21] Unto him be glory in the church by Christ Jesus throughout all ages, world without end. Amen.

APPENDIX 5 FOR:
5. LOVE – JUDGE NOT!

SEE TALKING POINTS: PAGE 53

Jesus Said

Matthew 7:14 Because strait is the gate, and narrow is the way, which leadeth unto life, and **few there be that find it.**

- ❑ On the one hand we take our eyes off of Jesus and look at those around us and say, "See me! See what I can do."

- ❑ On the other hand we take our eyes off of Jesus and look down and say, "Look at me…. I am a hopeless mess! I just can't do this! There is no hope for me….."

- ❑ Either way we run the risk of falling off of the narrow way and may become lost.

- ❑ Of course, it does not matter to Satan which way we go – as long as we are lost.

- ❑ The only way to stay on the path is to recognize our need and reach out to the Sunshine of God's love and ask Him to take over our lives – completely!

- ❑ We **<u>CANNOT</u>** do it alone!!

THE DANGER OF ANGER

Philippians 4:7 [NIV] And the peace of God, which transcends all understanding, will guard our hearts and our minds in Jesus Christ.

When I was in my 20's I went to a women's retreat. We heard a story from a lady who said that when she was young, she had to feed the chickens. She did not mind except for that one rooster. He was always pecking at her and making her so very angry. One day the thought came to her, "Do not be mad at the rooster." She went on to explain what anger can do to us.

Sadly, I did not heed this advice. I was always able to justify and make excuses for my anger. It was not until late in life that I finally realized why we are not to let anger take over. Anger blocks the Joy, the Sunshine of God's love. We all have "roosters" in our lives. Things we have no control over, things that hurt us, things that just do not go the way we think they must.

Problem is, we cannot hear "the still, small voice" if we are in turmoil. We cannot hear "the still small voice" if we are mad at the "rooster." **Do read the story of Elijah in I Kings 19.**

Let us allow that Joy, that Sunshine to burn away the anger.

CONTENTMENT

- Not to be content to do nothing! Not to be content to sit and stagnate and do nothing and cease to grow and flourish! NO!!

- But to have that firm foundation from which to grow and flourish. A foundation emotionally. A foundation spiritually. That calm luminosity inside of you. **Not wishing for more of what this world has to offer!**

- Yet we know – foundations need maintenance. We must constantly keep that connection to the Joy. We must spend time in our Secret Garden in order to have something to share. In order to not be wise in our wonderings.

What Paul says in Philippians 4:11-13

> [11]I am not saying this because I am in need, for I have learned to be content whatever the circumstances. [12]I know what it is to be in need, and I know what it is to have plenty. I have learned the secret of being content in any and every situation, whether well fed or hungry, whether living in plenty or in want. [13]I can do all this through him who gives me strength. [NIV]

APPENDIX 6 FOR: KEEP IT SIMPLE

SEE TALKING POINTS: PAGE 67

WHAT I EXTRAPOLATED FROM THE MOVIE *EAT, PRAY, LOVE*

EAT = PHYSICAL RESTORATION
- Rebuild and strengthen the vessel – our body and mind
- Jesus dined and relaxed with good friends

PRAY = SPIRITUAL RESTORATION
- Fill the repaired vessel with the Joy, the Sunshine – our mind and soul
- Jesus went away by Himself to be alone with God

LOVE = SHARING
- Share that Joy with others
- The very power of love flowed from Jesus to those around Him

APPENDIX 7: NOTES TO THE DISCUSSION LEADER(S)

NOTE DISCUSSION LEADER(S)

- The key word here is "**Guide**!" Pray before each session. Let the Joy in and follow where it leads you. Encourage discussion.

- Not all sections have an Appendix. Do not use them if they do not seem relevant to the direction your discussion is taking. Add your own when it will help you.

- This material can be used as a five week class or a workshop. Suggest 5, 45 minute sessions for a class setting (see Table of Contents) and 3, 3 hours sessions for a workshop. **For a workshop** use 1) Week One, 2) Weeks Two and Three, 3) Weeks Four and Five. Take time to do the Challenges as a group as time allows.

- **REGARDING PURCHASING AND PRINTING:** It is recommended that each student has a copy of *It Is Always NOW!* These may be purchased individually through Amazon or eBay.

- **For the *Study Guide* – For the Discussion Leader:** You need only purchase one for each discussion leader.

- **For the *Study Guide*:** Each student will need a copy of their own. These can be purchased on Amazon.

- OR – You can purchase a PDF version on eBay that can be printed multiple times for each study group.

NOTES ON SOME OF THE CHALLENGES:

NEW PATHWAYS – PAGE 25: NOTE TO INSTRUCTOR: Next week bring a shredder to class.

LOVE! JUDGE NOT! – PAGE 30: NOTE TO INSTRUCTOR: Have each participant tear out their one page from last week and shred it. **Emphasize** that this is not going to make this hurt, these feelings, go away. They are committing to building a new pathway. As long as they keep trying and asking for God's help, they will be right with God.

TRANSCEND – PAGE 34: NOTE TO INSTRUCTOR: Have each participant tear out their one page from last week and shred it. **Emphasize** that this is not going to make this hurt, these feelings, go away. They are committing to building a new pathway. As long as they keep trying and asking for God's help, they will be right with God.

Credits & Sources quoted from *100 Ways to Keep Your Soul Alive*

#3. Excerpt from p. 170 of *The Clown in the Belfry: Writings of Faith and Fiction* by Frederick Buechner. Copyright 1992 by Frederick Buechner. Reprinted by permission of HarperCollins Publishers, Inc.

#10. Hasidic tale. Quoted in *Peacemaking Day by Day*. Erie, PA: Pax Christi, 1985.

#15. John of Ruysbroeck. Quoted from *The Common Experience: Signposts on the Path to Enlightenment* by J. M. Cohen and J.F. Phipps. Wheaton, IS Quest Books, 1992.

#16. Shunryu Suzuki-roshi in *Zen Mind, Beginner's Mind*. New York: Weatherhill, 1970

#17. Brief quotation from *Family Tales, Family Wisdom: How to Gather the Stories of Lifetime and Share them with Your Family* by Dr. Robert U. Akeret with Daniel Klein. Copyright 1991 by Robert Akeret and Daniel Klein. Reprinted by permission of William Morrow & Company, Inc.

#29. Thomas Merton in *Contemplation in a World of Action*. Garden City, NY: Doubleday & Co., 1971 (p. 345)

#39. Rumi in *Unseen Rain, Quatrains if Rumi*. Translated by John Moyne and Coleman Barks. Putney, VT: Threshold Books, 1986. Reprinted by permission of Threshold Books, RD 4, Box 600, Putney, VT 05346.

#50. From *The Wisdom of Heschel* (excerpt from "Wonder… Radical…Amazement…Awe") by Abraham Joshua Herschel. Edited by Ruth Marcus Goodhill. New York: Farrar, Straus & Giroux, 1975.

#52. Joseph Gosse in "Inexhaustible Springs." *Spiritual Life* 36, 1 (Spring 1990).

#64. John Wellwood in *Ordinary Magic: Everyday Life as Spiritual Path*. Boston: Shambhala, 1992 (p. xiii).

#85. From *Endgame: A Journal of the Seventy-ninth Year* by ay Sarton. New York: W. W. Norton, 1972 (p. 250)

#98. Diane Ackerman in *A Natural History of the Senses*. Copyright 1990 by Diane Ackerman. New York: Random House, 1990.

To contact us or learn about our other book

See our website:
MardiLongBooks.com

www.ingramcontent.com/pod-product-compliance
Lightning Source LLC
LaVergne TN
LVHW070522070526
838199LV00072B/6680